Animals in the Forest

Élisabeth de Lambilly-Bresson

The Hedgehog

I am a hedgehog.
For safety,
I am covered with quills.
The minute I sense danger,
Yikes!
I roll myself into a ball.
I look like a pincushion
full of needles.

The Fox

I am a fox.
My fur is red.
My snout is long.
No noise escapes
my pointed ears.
I am clever. I am sly.
No prey escapes
my golden eyes.

The Deer

I am a deer.
I wear antlers like a crown.
The older I get,
the bigger they grow.
They help me
protect fawns and does
from danger.

The Wild Boar

I am a wild boar.
My coat has more hair
than my cousin, the pig's,
and its bristles
are much thicker.
I look for food
all night long,
and I eat everything!

The Owl

I am an owl.
When I call, I say Whooo!
With fringed feathers, I fly
silently.
I see well in the dark
with my big, round eyes,
so I hunt by night.
Look out, mice!

The Woodpecker

I am a woodpecker.
Such a noisy bird am I!
You can hear me
all over the forest.
Rat-a-tat-tat!
I drill holes in trees
with my pointed beak.

The Squirrel

I am a squirrel.
Watch me scamper up a tree!
I leap from branch to branch
as I gather nuts and seeds.
I chatter as I nibble.
I am quick to run away.
When I see another squirrel,
it is always time for play.

Please visit our Web site at: www.garethstevens.com
For a free color catalog describing Gareth Stevens Publishing's
list of high-quality books, call 1-800-542-2595 (USA) or
1-800-387-3178 (Canada).

Library of Congress Cataloging-in-Publication Data

Lambilly-Bresson, Elisabeth de.
    [Dans la forêt. English]
    Animals in the forest / Elisabeth de Lambilly-Bresson. — North American ed.
       p. cm. — (Animal show and tell)
    ISBN: 978-0-8368-8205-6 (lib. bdg.)
    1. Forest animals—Juvenile literature. I. Title.
QL112.L3313 2007
591.73—dc22   2007002553

This North American edition first published in 2008 by
Gareth Stevens Publishing
A Weekly Reader® Company
1 Reader's Digest Road
Pleasantville, NY 10570-7000 USA

Translation: Gini Holland
Gareth Stevens editor: Gini Holland
Gareth Stevens art direction and design: Tammy West

This edition copyright © 2008 by Gareth Stevens, Inc. Original edition copyright
© 2001 by Mango Jeunesse Press. First published as *Les animinis: Dans la forêt*
by Mango Jeunesse Press.

Printed in the United States of America

1 2 3 4 5 6 7 8 9 11 10 09 08 07